in no particular order

jaycina almond

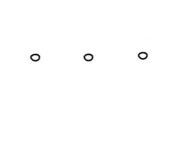

for myself + anybody else who has struggled to believe in themselves

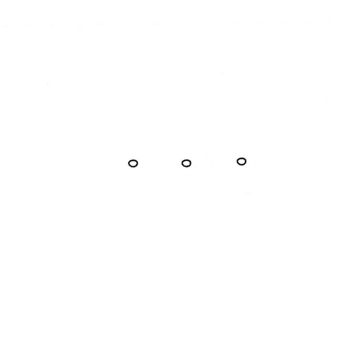

self-doubt is the swimming pool all the artists drown in

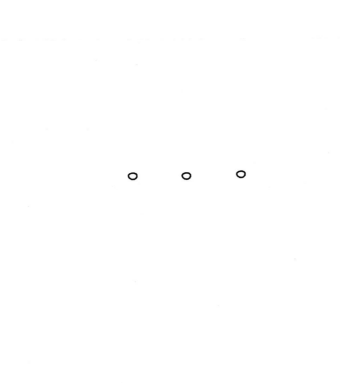

don't forget
i've been fire from the start
but now that i have burned you
arson isn't your thing

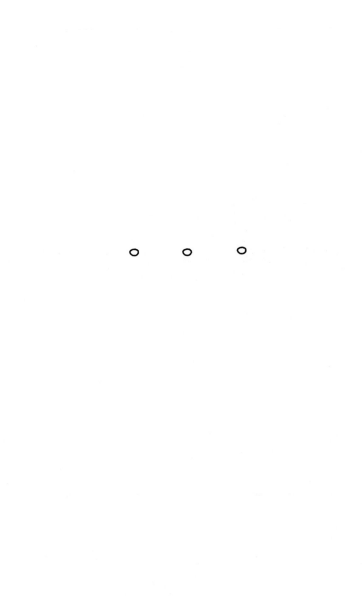

i blame my fire for a lot
i should probably choose people that enjoy hot climates and
know aloe vera heals even the biggest of burns

he doesn't realize she is addicted to fire and the only thing she
enjoys to see burn is herself

i know i said i enjoy setting myself on fire but maybe i'm tired
of arson
instead of burning
i'm ready to blossom

i bottle my emotions because i'm afraid if they oOze onto your
palms you'll decide to wash your hands

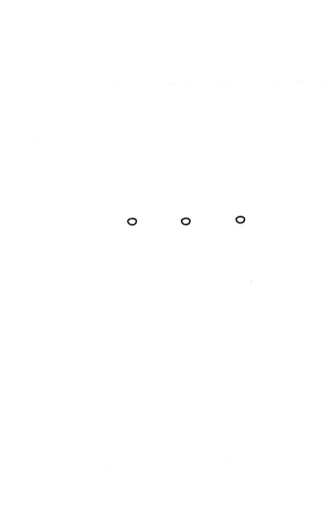

our love could burn whole cities down instead you chose me
i'm only ashes at your feet

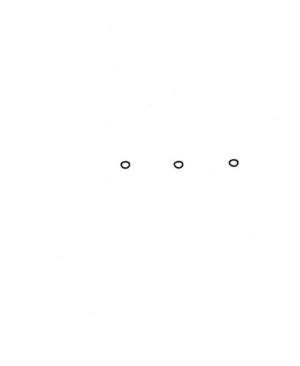

sometimes i know i am the sun until i remember the sun can
hide in the clouds and down here there is nowhere for me to
run

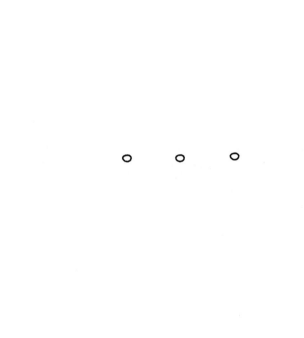

he can lick the fire from my bare lips
and watch
as flames rage inside me
i burn
then i cum
so now
his mouth is an ocean

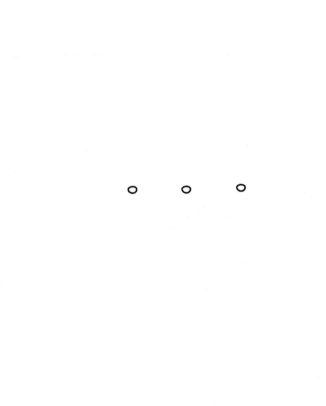

i got used to him always rescuing me
it was our thing in the beginning but he could never save me
from myself,
so when he gets tired of trying he'll whisper how i need him too
much

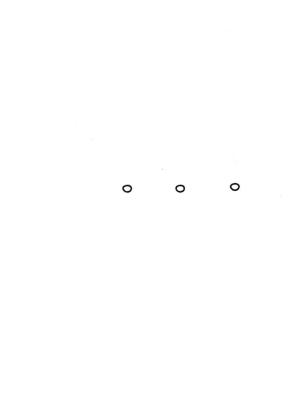

WHY I NEVER TOLD MY MOM HOW SHE BROKE MY HEART
OR WHY I WALKED ON A BROKEN LEG FOR 3 DAYS

i've been swallowing pain my whole life
keeping it tucked away behind the gap in my teeth and shoving
it back down my throat

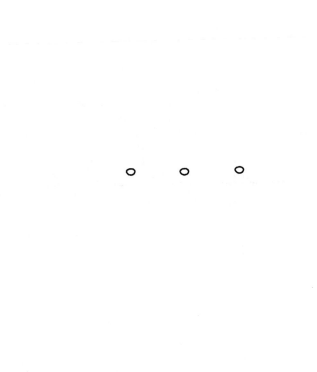

the caregiver's daughter
couldn't fix what he broke
that wound in her chest won't heal

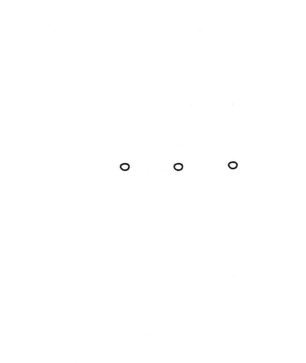

i changed my hair color and put holes in my face just to get
away from the girl he thought he missed

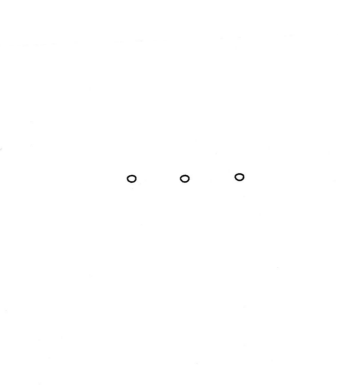

they say girls will marry men like their fathers but i never had
one of those and come to think of it
i've never met a man worth marrying either

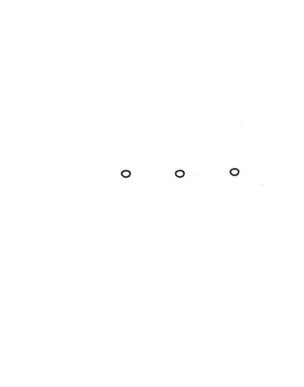

repeat after me: people are not medicine

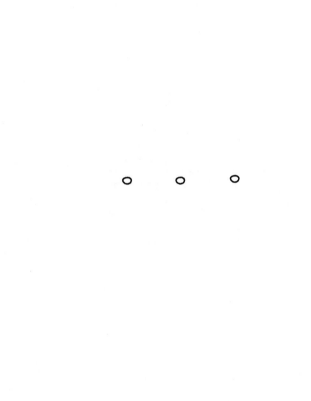

SIX WORD STORY

some old scars are self-inflicted.

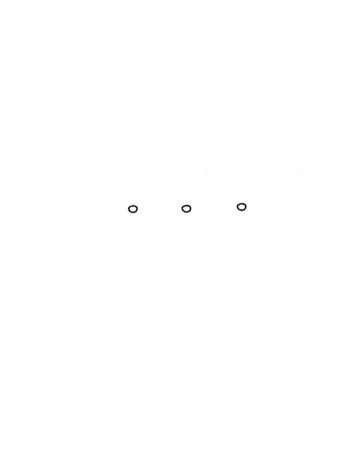

i know they say women have galaxies in them
but i got God in me

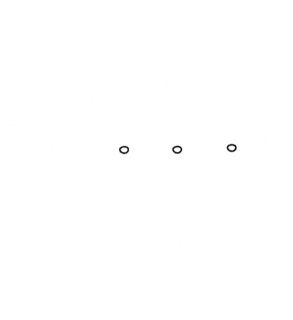

there is no men in my family
the women here only birth daughters
daughters that grow up with no fathers

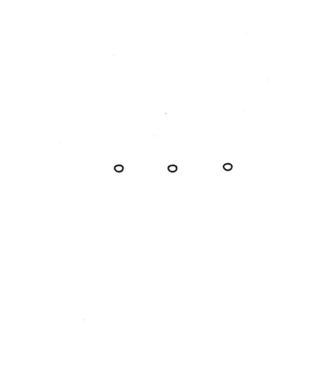

he said i was perfect but that was before he noticed the gap in
my teeth and my crooked pinkies

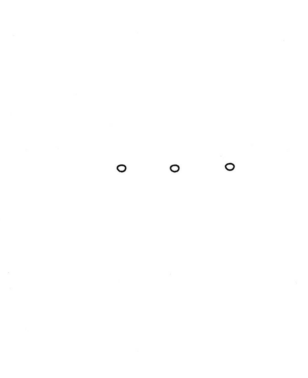

TEXTS I TYPED BUT DIDN'T SEND:

- please slow down, you're growing out of me

- she has your eyes

- why aren't you proud of me

- i stopped wearing the ring because it made me sad. it looked too much like a wedding ring

- i'm not as weak as you think

- i still think she is better for you

- sometimes i forget how to love myself, you knew that in the beginning though

- i'm glad it was dark when you called, you couldn't see my tears

- when did we become strangers? were we always?

he was perfect
for tight hugs and
teaching   detachment

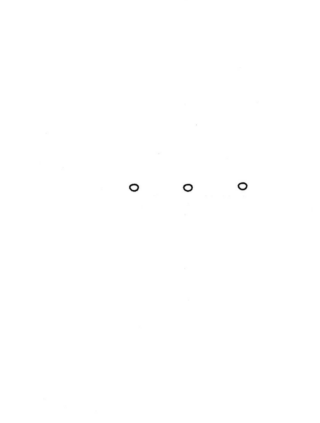

see, we didn't really fall in love, we crashed and consumed each other whole

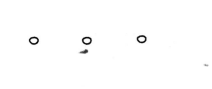

you can't go around making homes out of people
when bones will never be stronger than brick

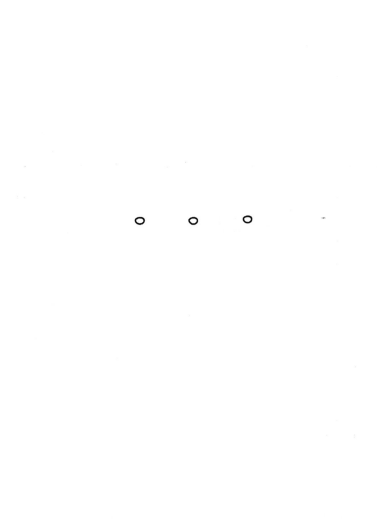

i was afraid of drowning in big bodies of water
not the kind with a heartbeat
so i dove right in and he swallowed me

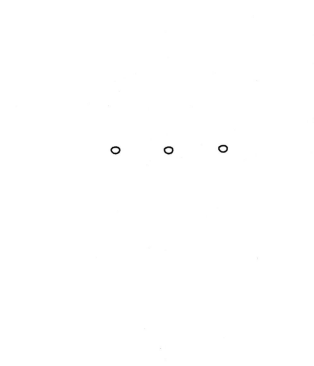

they told me you have the oceans inside of you i just figured
you would water me
and watch me grow
that was my first mistake, i asked for too much

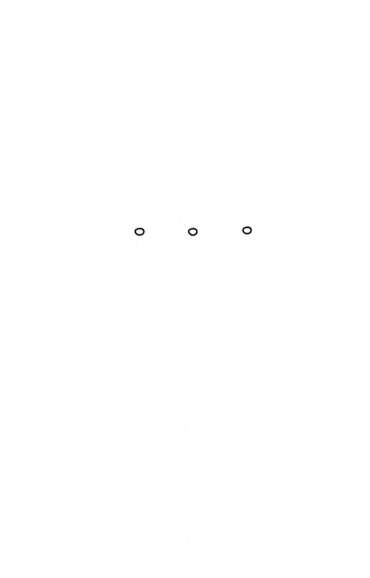

i've talked myself out of his love more times than i've believed
in it

RESENTMENT

resentment settles in and makes herself at home
in our bed

UNCERTAINTY

we stopped making plans for the future
when she showed up and joined resentment

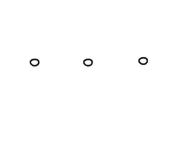

the only time i'm not fragile is when his hands are wrapped
around my neck

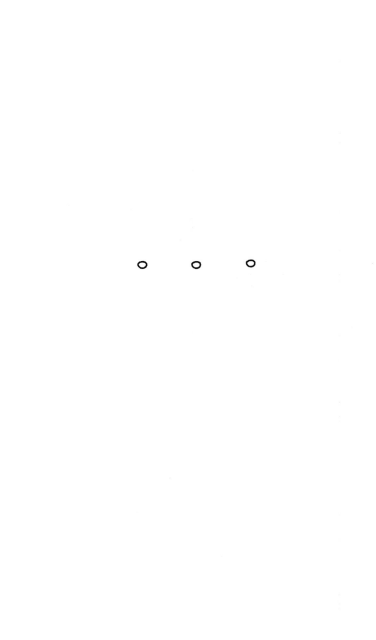

he never saw me as a poet sometimes i wanted to shove a fistful of my words down his throat and brand them onto his skin just to show him who i really am

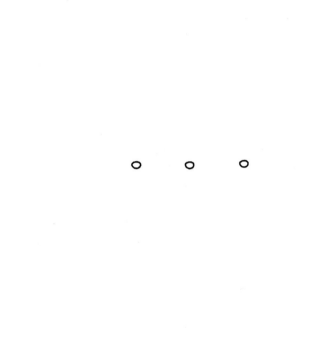

blood and bones are recycled
make sure to love the mothers still living in your hips

we'll tell her
you're what happens
when oceans part
and wildfires calm

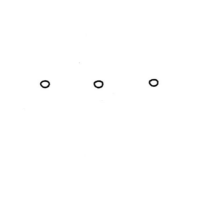

my mother was alone as she birthed me
my father dropped her off and left
i think i've been scared of men
who claim they love me,
leaving
ever since.

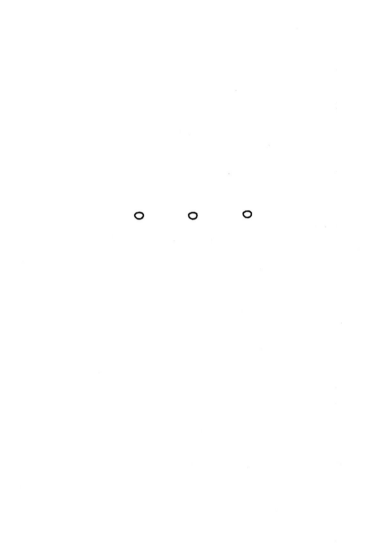

even oceans are known to dry out
just like love

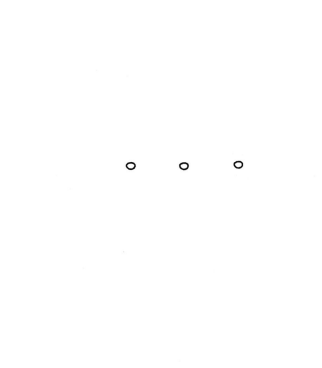

you'll wonder, when do i start releasing my mother's trauma
that has been stuck in my chest for decades so my own
daughter can grow a belly full of roses instead of sinking in
secondhand sorrow

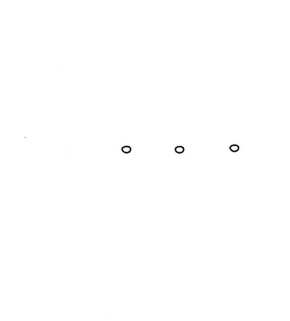

my heart is made out of fire and glass